"Greg Roeszler's character-based approach to coaching kids is very refreshing. He has a great perspective on what it means to be a role model and an athlete with sound values."

—*Tom Osborne, Athletic Director, University of Nebraska*

"I am COMPLETELY blown away by this work! What a great message for coaches—of ANY age. I am in awe of what you have done."

—*David Humm,*
Quarterback, Oakland/L.A. Raiders, Buffalo Bills, and Baltimore Colts 1975–84

"Watching the first half of the game from the box last night was brutal. I expected to see kids taking their frustration out on each other at halftime, kids who were thinking, *'Why am I even bothering to do this?'* Instead, Coach Lambdin asked me if I saw an opportunity for adjustments that would make us more competitive. I saw Coach Freeman calmly instructing the O line on simple adjustments in technique that would make a difference, and you were inspiring the kids to go out and have fun while competing and learning the game.

"The boys responded in a way that almost made me cry with emotion. I can't tell you how impressed I am with the character they have developed. They not only didn't quit, they truly thought they could win the second half—and went out and did it! Even though the other team was penalized a number of times for unsportsmanlike conduct, the Bulldogs maintained their poise throughout the game—unbelievable.

"Please let the kids know that last night they taught ME a lesson on working through adversity and not losing faith in oneself or one another. I'm very proud to be a part of their FAMILY."

—*Joe Bodnar, Assistant Coach, Encina High School, Folsom, California*

"What you are doing is great! Not only are you sending out a positive message to the rest of the students, you've put your players ahead of the game in terms of maturity. Thanks again!"

—*Robert Cowan, a Bulldog fan, Sacramento, California*

"What a great way to improve the status of athletics! These people are leaders on the field. By holding them responsible for their grades, and coaching them to be school leaders, you are doing a great thing."

—*Oliver Sasse, Consultant, Sacramento, California*

"I have observed Greg Roeszler with young people. I can assure you that the gifts, talents, and abilities this man has are quite rare. He focuses on equipping the total person—mind, body, and heart."

—*Betty Murakami, an Elementary School Teacher, Rancho Cordova, California*

"Coach Roz has assisted our organization in creating a vision that has made it possible for three of our teams to play for championship titles this year. He has been instrumental in creating opportunities for learning, while developing values which encourage self-discipline, teamwork, fair play and leadership skills. Coach Roz has supported our organization's aim to fulfill the needs of the community through a commitment to service while achieving excellence for coaches and parents in a fair and diverse environment.

"Coach Roz is the kind of leader people want to follow. His communication style is laced with patience and fueled with purpose. He empowers everyone around him and draws them forward. His vision becomes the team's vision.

"If asked to describe Coach Roz in one word, it would be *servant-hood*. Servant-hood is not about position or skill. It's about attitude, generosity, and giving oneself to others. Our youth have learned that true generosity isn't an occasional event. It comes from the heart and permeates every aspect of one's life, touching one's time, talents and possessions. This is the gift Coach Roz has given to me and the Sacramento Jr. Falcons Youth Football & Cheer Organization."

—*Deirdred (Dee Dee) Walsh, President,*
Sacramento Jr. Falcons Youth Football & Cheer Organization, Sacramento, California

"What a wonderful two days you have provided for the kids of San Marcos! I can't thank you all enough for what you have brought to our community through your football camp. Everyone had wonderful things to say. They really appreciated your message and your mission. Thanks again for everything!"

—*Kimberly Deutsch, a player's Mom, San Marcos, California*

"My success as a son, brother, player, coach, boyfriend, co-worker, and friend is attributed to the principles of family. My family includes my immediate family, the friends I chose, the teams I coach, the coaches and teachers and the people that took time to help me become the person I am today.

"Working together, having each others' backs, always being there for one another, regardless of the situation: these are some of the core principles we live by as family. Playmakers is all about that … family. The community, the teams we coach, and the lives we touch are part of our family. Together, the Playmakers organization is doing great things to make the people and the place where we live the best it can be."

—*Gino Moio, West Campus High School Football Coach, Sacramento, California*

"The concepts you have presented in this book are so easy to follow. They just make sense! These concepts will act as positive stepping stones which will allow both parents and children to soar. Thank you for everything you do. What you are doing is much larger than football and disadvantaged youth. It is about US, ALL of us."

—*Chelsea Mathieu, Curriculum Coordinator,*
Dept. of Family and Community Medicine, Sacramento, California

"This program has given at-risk kids a sense of self-worth, motivation, and achievement they've never had. Playmakers' model of good citizenship and camaraderie has literally transformed the lives of these young people and changed entire cultures on school campuses throughout California and beyond."

—*Lucia Churches, President, Ward Associates, Sacramento, California*

"Inner city kids normally do not go to football camps, so what Greg is doing is huge. Greg's camps are special because the coaches participate in the teaching, instead of just watching. Working with other teams, as well as our own, helps break down barriers between athletes from different schools. It gives kids a chance to see each other in a different light, not as enemies, but as football players who are part of a fraternity."

—*John Heffernan, Burbank High School Football Coach,*
Used by permission, Sacramento Bee

"Greg Roeszler is a great coach who understands his priorities—faith, family, and friends. He coaches to make a difference in young players' lives. This book is a reality check on why we coach. Greg reminds us that we need to be positive role models for our players, to be teachers first, coaches second."
—Frank Kalil, President, All American Youth Football, Corona, California

"Excellent points on all accounts. It made me think long and hard about some of the things I'm doing and some of the things I need to do. Great example of using Seniors as leaders in your program. Great perspective on what high school athletics should be. Love how you handle parents. (I will steal these ideas.) Many of my players are in very similar situations. You motivated me today. Can't wait to get to practice!!"
—Coach Bill Powell, Head Coach, Mt. San Jacinto High School,
Mt. San Jacinto, California

"Coach Roz shares his heart and real life experiences to help young men utilize football as a platform to develop what really counts—their hearts. In his book, Coach Roz shares tips and anecdotes that will help all athletes, coaches, and parents develop their hearts and character, so you can be a leader in your family, community, and beyond. Today, our society is missing leaders that lead by serving first. Coach Roz teaches about the strongest form of leadership in the world—Servant Leadership. Thanks for sharing your heart, Coach Roz."
—Coach Chris Berg, Oak Park, California,
"Inspiration for the NEXT Generation"
www.CoachChrisBerg.com

"Wow! What a dynamic book! During my years working the "beat" as a Police Officer, I would have loved to have had this type of resource to share with parents who were struggling with their children. The situations, quotes, and problem solving techniques in this book would have made it so much easier to get my point across to kids and parents alike. Working with kids for the better part of twenty five years, mostly during negative or devastating situations, this book would have been invaluable by providing families proven lessons in life skills, character building ("doing the right thing when no one is watching"), and respect for self and others, just to name a few. I also believe this book is, and will be, instrumental in bridging the gap that often exists in relationships between parents and their children.

"Coach Roz and I have always shared a passion for the philosophy—'*We need to reach our youth before we have to rescue them.*' This book is one more resource that will help us all reach that goal by providing the tools and resources needed to remedy most problems associated with growing up and being a kid. Whether you're a parent, a student leader, a teacher, a coach, a police officer, or anyone else dealing with kids, this is a huge step in the right direction.

"I have been blessed to know Coach Roz and to have had the opportunity to learn many lessons from him myself.

"Roz, I am so proud to see you have the opportunity to '*GO DEEP*' once again by placing your heart and soul into this great book. All my best!!"

—*Jeff Penn, Director of Operations-Southern California,*
California Police Youth Charities.

Coaching for a BIGGER Win

A Playbook for Coaches

Coaching for a
BIGGER
A Playbook for Coaches
Win

Greg "Coach Roz" Roeszler
with Donna Miesbach

PLAYMAKERS™
PRESS
Rancho Cordova, California

The names of all the students mentioned in this book have been changed. Their stories have not.

Quote on page 9 taken from *Quiet Strength* by Tony Dungy and Nathan Whitaker. © 2007 by Tony Dungy. Used by permission of Tyndale House Publisher, Inc. All rights reserved.

On the cover: Playmakers Free Summer Football Camps are for children ranging in age from seven to nineteen. Each year some child emerges who touches your heart in a special way. These kids become Coach Roz's helper and get a shoulder ride throughout the camp. The shoulder rides began when the little boy in this picture didn't want to stay. He felt overwhelmed by how many children were there and told Coach Roz he'd really rather go home. Roz picked the boy up and put him on his shoulders. That helped a little, but he still wasn't sure he wanted to stay, so Roz made him an Assistant Coach and gave him jobs to do. From that point on, the boy loved the camp and stayed all three days.

ISBN13: 978-0-9822514-1-6
ISBN10: 0-9822514-1-6
Library of Congress Control Number: 2008942019
Cataloging in Publication Data on file with publisher.

Playmakers Press
A Division of Playmakers Mentoring Foundation
P.O. Box 728
Rancho Cordova, CA 95741
(916) 220-1284
E-mail: CoachRoz@ThePlaymakers.org

Editorial Services: Donna Miesbach
Book Design & Layout: Gary James Withrow
Marketing & Publicity: Concierge Marketing, Inc.

Printed in the United States of America
10 9 8 7 6 5 4 3 2 1

Contents

Dedication

To the heroes in my life: Hummer,* Uncle Lyle, Ron "Bull," and Tree Plumbtree, who is teaching me how to coach. Thank you, each one, for where you are in my heart.

To my Dad, a real hero, who coaches me on how to be a Father. I can't do it like you did, but I try. I am proud to be called "Roy's son."

*David Humm

Acknowledgments

I am so grateful for all the coaches who have shaped me—Gus Nolan, my youth coach, who believed in me. Coach Schwartz, my high school coach, who tried to shape me when I wanted nothing to do with being shaped. Rick Garretson, who mentors and coaches me each week and is a tremendous friend. Tree Plumbtree, who just inspires me in so many ways. Tree, you are a great coach, teacher, and man. Lorenzo Walsh, who fights the battle in "the hood," championing the cause for lost kids. Coach Braio, who teaches me how to serve others and how to live well.

My thanks to all of you who have allowed me into the fraternity. And lastly, to the next coach who is willing to go the distance with these kids. If I can help, I'm in your corner.

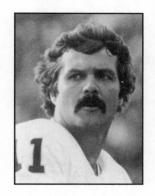

Foreword

When it comes time for our children to play in a sport, every parent wants their children to have the best experience they can possibly have, whether we played in a sport or not.

Coach Roz's book, *Coaching for a Bigger Win, A Playbook for Coaches,* will give you a roadmap to success that takes you through the tryout stage, to making the team, and what goes on during the season. Not only that, Coach Roz makes it fun for all.

It is so important to make sure children get the rest and nutrition they need, not only so they can be physically fit throughout the year, but also so they can be ready for all that will come their way as they grow and mature. Coach Roz lays out these steps so your program can be a success for parents and athletes alike. This book will serve as your Game Plan so you can make sports enjoyable for both parents and their kids.

Roz's methods are profound, yet they are simple and they are fun. Roz speaks with many years of experience. Coach Roz and his staff have drawn on the best and used that knowledge to build a successful program in the most difficult arena of all—the inner city.

These are the best years of our children's lives. Here is a way to make those years a fun time while teaching them great life lessons. This book is definitely worth the read.

Thanks, Coach Roz and your staff! Let's "PLAY BALL!!"

—*David Humm*
Quarterback, Oakland/L.A. Raiders, Buffalo Bills, and Baltimore Colts 1975–84

Introduction

As I began my journey into coaching many years after my playing days were over, I wasn't sure exactly where that road was going to take me. Looking back, I am so grateful that I got on that road. Coaching has given me a focus for how I will spend my remaining years and, hopefully, finish life well.

Little did I know, when I began what was a weekend hobby, that it would turn into what appears to be my destiny and my life's passion. So here is a word of caution: Be careful as you enter into this great fraternity of coaches, as it can transform you, *if* you are coachable, into the man you were destined to be.

I am only just now realizing the impact we youth and high school coaches have on the community we live in. Our Playmakers Mentoring Foundation has linked men with little common socio-economic background together in magnificent ways.

What began as merely a football camp mushroomed into an organization involved in mentoring, teaching accountability and masculine life skills to fatherless youth. From there, Playmakers began assisting single Moms in the awesome task of raising a child alone. Then we began working with kids in group homes, creating trust and a team environment.

Through this task of mentoring youth and serving in the community, we are beginning to understand and love men of different colors and circumstances more. As a result, kids from different neighborhoods are playing and serving in the community side by side as they learn about caring for one another.

Because we have gotten kids to work together in causes larger than themselves, pastors and congregations of different churches are reaching out to help us.

So a "hobby" has turned into a mission of mentoring kids and coaching coaches on how to love kids and make them leaders in the community. We are crafting young men and giving them a Game Plan on how to be a good Husband and Father when that time comes. We are laying a foundation for them in the hope that they will not leave their families, that they will go the distance, and that they can be counted on for a lifetime.

We are using the football field as the "classroom" to get that job done. Football will not cure cancer, but it can be a vehicle that can change the trajectory of a lost kid who desperately needs a coach in his life to show him the way. Over time, that memory, and that relationship, will be hardwired into that young man's soul.

Here is the bonus for all of this. For me, coaching football has been a redemption in so many ways. It is giving me a Game Plan for being a better man, Husband, and Father. It is teaching me about character and about how to mentor kids and parents who desperately need us.

Be careful if you truly enter into this venture 100%. Coaching will bring you kids and parents who are looking for leadership. It will raise your personal accountability to a new level. Coaching could even lead you to seek redemption from the scars you may have with your own Dad, and bring you or some young man to a new level of healing and understanding.

I honor you for entering into these challenges, and I look forward to journeying with you.

—Coach Roz

A deal is a deal!

Men of Integrity

One of the finest humans I know is Tree Plumbtree. He is one of my mentors who has taught me a great deal about football, and even more about life. Tree and I have known each other since we were kids at rival high schools. I kicked a field goal in 1974 that kept his team from shutting us out, and we still laugh about it today. He has forgotten more about football than I will ever know. Our relationship spans over thirty years, and it is getting even better as time goes by.

Tree not only teaches the toughest and most academically challenged kids his school can find, he makes students out of them. I personally watched him beat Stage Four cancer two years ago. He is one of the toughest men I have ever met; I honestly believe Squamous Cell Carcinoma was afraid of him. During that time, we e-mailed and talked almost daily. Tree showed me what you can achieve when your heart and mind tell your body you are not done yet.

Tree is a man of deep integrity. When he gives his word or commitment to something, you can go to the bank with it. We have spent hours on the lake bass fishing and just talking about life, coaching, and mentoring kids. (Tree is an expert bass fisherman, too. He is too obsessive to do anything less than perfect.) I get inspired just writing about Tree. He has given me so many tools to make kids better men.

Tree has a pretty simple rule when it comes to an agreement. When he says he is going to do something, he does it. You know you can count on him because he does what he says he is going to do. Tree expects the same in return. If he gets anything less than your best effort, he will let you know because, as Tree says, "A deal is a deal." There are countless high school coaches throughout California who can tell you how Tree Plumbtree has influenced their lives. He is a great man of integrity, and I owe him so much.

See you on the bass lake, Hoss, and I'll try not to fall out of the boat ... again.

What is the
best team
I've coached?

Ask me in twenty
years when we see
what kind of men
they've become.

Define True Success

I wish I was profound enough to have made that quote up, but I'm not. It comes from the legendary coach of Penn State's Nittaney Lions, Joe Paterno. Coach Paterno is known as a great man who cares about what kind of man you have become by playing football.

Joe Paterno is eighty-one years young and is beginning his fifty-ninth season at Penn State. What I would give just to sit and talk to Joe Paterno about staying the course and not quitting! Fifty-nine years at the same job! In a society where we change jobs for another $1.00 an hour raise, Joe has been at the same job in the same place for over fifty years! Could Joe Paterno teach people something about longevity and endurance? I think so. I also think that Joe Paterno probably has something to say to people who believe they are too old for something.

I can only imagine what a reunion looks like when you played for Coach Paterno at Penn State. His portfolio includes some of the greatest linebackers who have played both in college and professionally. We call his school

"Linebacker U." He has coached National Championship Teams and is in the same category with "The Bear" and Bobby Bowden.

You see, Coach Paterno judges his success by how many men of character he has put into society. Now, all coaches say that is important, but Coach Paterno lives it. He equates success with whether or not he has been a positive influence on the young men he coaches.

What kind of legacy do you think Coach Paterno is leaving? How many players has he impacted? Ten? One hundred? A thousand, or more? How many coaches have grown from his "coaching tree"? How does Joe Paterno shape men of character and teach them how to become Husbands and Fathers of character? I hope I get to meet Mr. Paterno so I can just sit with him and learn. The coaching fraternity is an awesome brotherhood where most coaches are willing to share what they have learned about the game. When I get my chance, I just want to ask Mr. Paterno how to make young men better men.

*Listen carefully!
This is as loud
as I am going
to talk.*

Have Character

Tony Dungy gets the credit for this one. Tony is such a man of faith and character. I met Tony when we were both quarterbacks at the University of Minnesota. He was the starting quarterback my freshman and sophomore year. As a backup, I sat on the bench and watched him become a great player when The Big Ten actually had ten schools.

From the day you met Tony Dungy, you knew he was special. He was special in the classroom and on the field. When I was in college, watching Tony was like having another coach on the field.

Much has been written about Tony, and his book, *Quiet Strength: The Principles, Practices, & Priorities of a Winning Life* (co-authored with Nathan Whitaker and Denzel Washington), is one of the best books I've read. It gives you a glimpse into his strength and faith. Every football coach should make that book, along with *Season of Life: A Football Star, a Boy, a Journey to Manhood* (by Jeffrey Marx), the core of their coaching library. As coaches, most of us have books on everything from "The Spread Offense" to "Defending the Wing T." Too few of us have books in our library on shaping men and effective communication. We should be reading material that will actually give us life skills we can teach.

It is well documented that Tony Dungy is a quiet man. You do not see Tony berating a player or ranting and raving on the sidelines about a bad call. Maybe Tony just doesn't get bad calls or have a player miss an assignment. As a coach who yells too much (me), I aspire to be more like Tony. I aspire to have his sideline conduct. I aspire to be the communicator that he is, and I aspire to be the man of faith that he is.

How are these things going to happen? As a coach, they must become a "value." They must be among your non-negotiables. You must read, attend coaching clinics, and be coachable to change. Too many of us say, "This is how I coach." Is this how you are a Husband, or how you parent or lead kids? As coaches, we MUST be willing to change how we communicate with our kids. Be willing to read, study, and be coachable on being a better communicator. I have not attended one coach's clinic where the topic is "Yelling Louder to Win." Youth coaches, times have changed. Just because your high school coach was loud, that does not mean that is how you must coach.

Is that your
best effort?

Create a Fair Playing Field

I think I need to give credit to Tree Plumbtree for this one, too, although I am sure he stole it from someone. Tree played for El Camino High School, and I played for Encina, where I now coach. El Camino and Encina were rivals, and we still talk about those games. High school football is hardwired into most of us coaches.

In case you don't know, Tree stands six feet three inches and will admit to two-hundred-fifty pounds. He is a former steer wrestler on the professional rodeo tour, and as a young man, there was not a fist fight he could avoid. The point is, he can blow your hair back, if he needs to. He is also a master at non-verbal communication.

I learn so much from him each time we get together, on the field or off. Like all of us, Tree is a very competitive coach who demands that things are done in an appropriate fashion. Tree tells us coaches to holler only when we are happy. He just does not believe in negative reinforcement, because "it rarely works." Because he is such a great teacher and coach, he instructs by drawing on his students' own inner strength, instead of relying on their fear of their coach or teacher.

You don't have to coach very long before you realize that kids have different abilities and interests in football. As one of my coaching buddies says, "We coaches spend countless hours preparing our Game Plan, and then we leave it in the hands of a sixteen-year-old kid." How true that is. Sometimes we coaches forget what we are asking kids to do.

We coaches all look for perfection and great execution on the field and in the classroom. We tell kids their effort or result is just not good enough time after time. We are looking for a result that manifests on the scoreboard or on the report card. Tree doesn't do that. He simply says, "Son, is that your best effort?" That is such a fair yardstick for achievement. Usually, the kids will be brutally honest with you when you ask this question. They know if they are giving you their best in the classroom, on the field, or in the community. That question keeps their achievement on a fair playing field and teaches them a valuable life skill.

As a coach, there is nothing that gives us more pride and sense of accomplishment than when a kid gives you his or her best effort. That is all you can ask for. If I know that my team gave their best effort, I can tolerate and find great satisfaction in their effort, even while getting "rolled." (That's football lingo for being beaten soundly.)

Giving your best effort carries over to serving in the community as well. For example, each day our football team is completely responsible for cleaning the lunch room and picking up trash in the quad. This is not done as any form of punishment but simply because we are Playmakers. I love to see it when they give their best effort at lunch in the quad.

*You don't need a
personal trainer;
you need a tutor.*

Become a Family

Don't get me started about personal trainers in high school. David Humm (who is one of my heroes and one of Nebraska's all-time greatest quarterbacks) has made a career out of the game of football, and he, like me, had no personal trainer or personal highlight film. I wonder how he made it to the Oakland Raiders, Buffalo Bills, and Baltimore Colts.

We need to raise our kids' GPAs. My kids need to be tutored, not to have someone assist them with their ab crunches. If a coach can learn how to work their kids out better, those players will be just fine. With no disrespect to personal trainers, there are plenty of overweight people who can be fashionable by talking about their personal trainers, but you won't find personal trainers around our team. Our pride comes from bragging about how one of our girl volleyball players is assisting us in tutoring the freshmen. I am real proud of that, and you can be sure our team will be at her volleyball game yelling for her.

Coach, get creative, and get the grades up. You can recruit several tutors on campus, if you just make it a priority to do so. You can create something that will be the talk of your administration, just like it is on Encina's campus.

Another place you can find tutors is on your team. Our kids tutor each other. We are a family, and we have to depend on each other more often than kids at other schools. We are fine with that.

Let's look ahead at the ten-year class reunion. I can't wait to be there. I don't think the conversation is going to be, "Coach, do you remember the personal trainer you recommended to me? He got my 40 down to 4.6." I hope the conversation is something like this: "Coach, I remember the 6:45 study skills mornings, and how we cared about each other." I am going to meet people at that reunion who are successful Fathers and Husbands. Someone Far Greater than any of us will be keeping track of their personal highlight film, and it will be a fun one to see.

Stand for the anthem
at all the games;
you'll understand why
when you are a Dad.

Life Lessons

Where have all our traditions gone? Let me give you some startling observations. When I ask our kids what their Dad does for a living, not too many know. I know what you are thinking—that is in the inner city. But I tell you this, ask your son what he thinks you do for a living. You may be surprised at what you hear.

I think one of our jobs is to keep our history alive. Very few of our kids today know what Veteran's Day is all about. As coaches, we have an opportunity to be great teachers. 9-11 is burned into our minds if we are adults, yet my kids have little memory of it and its impact. They need to know about 9-11. They need to know there were four planes (not three) that went down. They need to know about Todd Beamer, and how he led his "team" to take over the cockpit and keep that plane from flying into our nation's Capitol. They need to know the lessons of "others first" that Pat Tillman demonstrated when he gave up pro football to defend our country.

These are just a few of the lessons that can be learned through football when a history teacher isn't getting through. I want my kids to be silent, standing tall, looking at that flag during the anthem. It is part of being a Playmaker and a coach. They are going to stand like I stand. Being in this country is a privilege, and so is playing football.

We do a drill at the end of each game called "The Hut Drill." It was taught to me by Rick Garretson, one of the best football coaches and friends a guy could have. We do the drill he taught me at the end of each game, win or lose. It is a disciplined drill where we face the crowd and do a combination of push-ups, sit-ups, and agility drills with Marine-like precision. The drill is our Playmakers' way of saying "Thank you" to the parents and alumni who have come to watch us. I hope that thirty years from now "The Hut Drill" is being done all across the country.

I heard your prayer; I just don't care who wins the game.

Keep It in Perspective

This quote should be on every coach's desk. I think it best sums up where our priorities should be. One of the best coaches I know is Rick Garretson. He has coached almost twenty years in one of the state's most competitive conferences in Orange County. He has had great success in shaping kids. He clearly states that he refuses to allow his identity as Husband and Father to be caught up in his win/loss record. This comes from one of the most competitive men I know.

Rick's brother, Ron, one of the NBA's best officials who also coaches youth football, said to me, "As coaches, we forget that the other team wants to win as much as you do." That is simple, yet so true. What we teach our kids after a loss is critical, and your words must be chosen carefully. Kids do not deserve to be in counseling as adults because you "hung" the loss on the defense, or you blamed a kid who does not live and die the game the way you do.

Make the game, A GAME. We are not curing cancer here (but one of our kids may cure it). We are shaping young men into adulthood. We are teaching masculinity and manhood in the truest sense. The game is just the practice field for the bigger picture. The question is, Coach, do you really believe in the bigger picture? If you do, I have an idea for you to consider.

Who have you selected for your staff because they are great mentors and men of character? I am privileged to have four coaches who have *zero* years experience coaching, and I could give a rip about that. They are there because I need men on my staff who care about kids 24-7. They walk that walk. They drive kids home from practice each night, and that is where they learn about our players. That is where they are learning to love our guys. We will figure out how to stop the "Wing T" along the way.

*Coach better
so every kid
gets in the game.*

Love Them Enough to Play Them All

One of the things that I am most proud of is this: EVERY kid who suits up plays every game. Now understand that I do not coach for a team that is going to be the National Champion, but you probably don't either. I coach for a team that is playing so every kid can get in the game, and we are getting better. I had a coach, who got carried away by the excitement of us winning a game, tell me, "Coach, if I keep the starters in, we can preserve a shutout!" We only had to have that conversation once. He just got caught up in the moment, but we got that all worked out. I want to convince every coach that *every kid should play.* That is one of my goals.

What character message are you sending to a kid who comes to practice every day and gives you his best effort to make the team better, yet he does not get dirty on game night? Do you really buy into the fact that "the win," and him just being "on the team," is enough? We're helping this kid enter manhood! He enters it by getting into the battle and getting dirty. I truly believe that if EVERY kid plays, we won.

Aunt Jennie and Nana came to the game to see their grandson and nephew play. Their memories will be that of their grandson being the star of the four plays you got him in and the special teams he played on. You know this is true. You just have to decide if "keeping the score close" is really important when you are getting rolled up. Let the other team put two more touchdowns on you and make sure everyone got in the game.

For the coach who says, "I don't want to put him in because he might get hurt," I tell you, COACH BETTER! Very rarely does a kid get hurt because he is too small. Put the kid on a special team, or put him in as a defensive back or wide receiver. At the end of the game, it just doesn't matter. If you are a really good coach, get him in earlier in the game.

Coach Moyer is our Personal Coach, and one of his jobs is to keep me informed on who has not yet been in the game. Win, lose, or draw (I hate that expression), I do not have to apologize at the end of the game to any kid because, in the heat of the battle, I just forgot to get him in the game.

*What's our job
as coaches?
"To care for us!"*

*What's your job
as Playmakers?
"To care for
each other!"**

Change the Kids' Trajectory

Joe Ehrmann's story, *Season of Life,* is my blueprint for coaching. I had the privilege of meeting Joe a couple of years ago. He left me feeling truly inspired. We shared breakfast together and just talked about mentoring kids. Joe is truly a great man. This quote was inspired by Joe and what he does with his teams. We have made this quote our Playmakers mantra, and in the summer of 2008, over 700 kids chanted it at our Playmakers camps.

Our kids need to know that caring for each other is *their job.* They need to learn that fact and do their jobs well. As coaches, we have a job, too. It is to *care about our players.* This may sound like any other team across the nation, but as Playmakers at Encina, we put teeth into it.

Each week, our kids must call and check in with us coaches. They usually do this on Sunday because we actually want to know if our kids made it through the weekend. In the inner city, this is just not a given. I am writing this at one o'clock in the afternoon. This morning we sat in the Catholic Cathedral at the funeral of a kid who attended a Playmakers camp the previous summer. He will not play again, because last weekend he was shot in the back of the head by a fifteen-year-old kid. This is why we check in. That puts teeth in caring about each other.

How else do we care about each other? After the funeral I took three of the kids to breakfast, and we just talked. I told them it is their "job" to let me know when there is a player in the family who has no place to live and is homeless. We need to know that fast so we can get them to a coach's house and make sure they have something to eat. Two of the kids at that breakfast shared that at one time they were homeless, too.

If you live in the suburbs, you may be thinking, "I can't believe this is really true," but if you are an inner city coach, you most likely have several kids just like the ones I am describing to you.

Playmakers make a difference. We link these lost kids with caring people, and businesses, and dedicated coaches who will stay the course with them.

*My deep appreciation to Joe Ehrmann for the idea for this quote!

*You've earned
the right to be last.*

Modeling Fatherhood

When I first began coaching kids "in the hood," seeing the void our fatherless society has created just about broke my heart. Our kids have little to no roadmaps, nor do they have a positive model of what a Dad actually looks like, so we had to create some situations where they could learn how to be a Dad. That's why our seniors are the Dads of our team, and here is what that looks like.

Freshmen usually have very few privileges. They are pushed to the back of the line. They are given the poorest equipment and no respect. That is just the way it has been in the high school pecking order. Not as a Playmaker, and not at Encina!

In homes across the country, when there is not enough food in the house, *Dads eat last.* Dads make sure that their family is taken care of first. It is the same with us. Last night we had our Parent/Player barbecue. I was so proud to hear the seniors say, "You parents eat first; then the freshmen can go. We'll eat last." That may be one of their first practical lessons on what it means to be a Dad who puts his family first.

On the practice field, many times the seniors will carry the bags in and out of the shed. They do it with good hearts and not with an attitude, because that is how they are coached. I look to the seniors (the Dads) and hold them accountable for language and character on the field. On more than one occasion, they have "gone to the track" because a freshman embarrassed the family.

As coaches, we are the Dads of the team also, and there are times that we coaches make mistakes or wrong decisions. I hope I am not the only coach who has chewed out a kid only to find out I had the wrong information. This is where you have an opportunity to teach a life lesson by getting in front of your team and saying I AM SORRY, and asking for forgiveness. Kids need to see a Dad say he was wrong and ask for forgiveness. Coach, when was the last time you got in front of your team and said, "I am sorry"? Teach Fatherhood through football. You have earned the right to be last, because Dads eat last in the family.

If you can't tell me your GPA, you're probably not too proud of it.

Hold Them Accountable

When you ask a baseball player about his batting average, if he's batting below .200, he will tell you, "I am hitting (about) .230." A player hitting over .300 will tell you, "I am hitting .312." It's funny when a player will round off, and when he knows to the one hundredth. The same is true about GPAs. Some kids will tell me, "It's (around) a 2.3." My 4.0 kids will tell me, "It's 4.28, Coach."

At the start of football season, we will have our first rally. Usually the coach will get in front of the entire student body and introduce the team of the decade. Our rally at Encina is a bit different, as it is led by our captains who will then give the microphone to each player who will, in front of the entire campus, introduce himself, give his grade, position, and CURRENT GPA. This is how we make grades a value. It's also how we send a message to our teachers about what is most important to the family.

When I talk to a kid who is struggling with a class, I tell him, "Son, we are going to go to your teacher right now, and I am going to ask her where you are sitting and are you giving your best effort." Here is the important part. Then I say, "What is SHE going to tell me?" That is a great starting point for improving in class. We don't start with "extra credit" assignments; we begin with "get current" assignments. Our kids will get current, even if they get no credit for it. We're teaching character, not the quickest way to get eligible.

Let's get back to the rally for a moment. Teachers have to go to the rallies, even though it may not be their favorite thing to do. My guess is that rarely is a rally a moment they'll want to write about in their journal. Here is how our rallies are different. You won't see our kids in their game jerseys at the rally. You WILL see them wearing neckties as they announce their grades to the student body. Never have I had a teacher tell me how great my team looked in sagging jeans and a jersey half tucked in sporting a dew rag, skull cap, and an earring. I have had comments that they looked classy in a tie, announcing their grades. We have no dew rags or skull caps, and definitely no earrings on our team.

*You **must** edify a kid who was cut!*

It Takes Many to Make a Family

I have not had to cut a kid yet. I know that when you, as a coach, are lucky enough to have more players than equipment, there may be a time where cuts have to be made. It just has not happened in my coaching universe. How a cut is handled is crucial when you are a Playmakers coach.

We teach the word *edify* throughout the year. By this I mean that we, as Playmakers, are constantly building one another up and breathing encouragement to one another. This is edifying the Playmakers' way. We teach this at homecoming when we give examples of how girls should be respected and honored.

Kids who do not make the team need to be edified and encouraged and given meaningful assignments so they are still part of the family. Here is my suggestion: No kid is EVER cut. There may be times where not every kid gets a uniform and plays on Friday night, but that kid IS part of the team. If you lay that foundation early, you should not lose a kid. He just may be serving the team in a different capacity. If the kid tells you that if he does not get a uniform, he quits, then you know what kind of character is lacking, and you won't depend on him anyway.

We have coaches' assistants that help every day. There are game day and game night activities that include stats, spotting in the booth, equipment, and videoing. These are just a few possible assignments. If you get creative, you can come up with enough activities to keep twenty kids busy, if you have created something the kids want to be part of. Have you done that?

Youth coaches, if you must cut a kid, there is only one way to do it, as far as I am concerned. You go to that kid's home and make it clear that you need him to help in many different ways. You need to make it clear that you, as a coach, are helping him get ready for NEXT season. Be there for them. I can promise you they are going to remember their first cut for a lifetime.

We're going to spend about 300 hours with your son this season.

Coach the Parents, Too

Last night we had our first parents' meeting, and we had thirty "guardians" there. A parent told me last year only two people came. We are making progress. This is where I "coach" parents on what I expect. I tell them that if they are going to use pulling their son off the team as a motivation for good behavior, they should take their son home *now,* as that is unacceptable, and I will not support that as a solution. We need to work on the problem together. We can get the result we are looking for by keeping the kid on the team where he can lose other privileges that may be important to him, including playing time.

Parents need to understand that football is not a democracy. It is, at times, a dictatorship. It is a privilege, not a right, to play football for Encina. This is exactly how I explain it to the parents, and if you don't believe it, come to one of our meetings. Parents can talk to me about how their son is doing in class, how he is doing in the community, and any problems he may have, but they CANNOT discuss playing time with me. NO EXCEPTIONS. It should be enough that every kid plays every game. Their son usually knows why he is or isn't starting or getting more playing time. Let's talk about character and other subjects that are more important than how many carries he got.

Parents (usually Dads) will often offer their opinions on everything from what offense we should run to what time practice should be over. Here is the heart of my talk on this subject: "Parents, we are going to spend about 300 hours with your son this season, including practice, coaches' meetings, tutoring, and games. If you are willing to put in the same 300 hours with us, then your opinion counts. If not, then it doesn't." And that's exactly how I say it.

Here is a talk that may be helpful to you when dealing with Dad. "Dad, have you played the game at a 'higher' level?" Most Dads will fall into the trap and answer, YES, I HAVE! "Then you know very well, as a Dad who has played at a higher level, that you cannot do what you are doing." If they have NOT played at a higher level (very few will admit they have not), you can now offer to "coach them up" on what is acceptable behavior.

Every one of us has seen a bad situation from a parent (usually a Dad) who is "too critical" of the play calling. When that happens, parents have a responsibility to handle the problem. We discuss this at the parents' meeting, and then we put a plan into action. It begins with a group of volunteer Dads who will tap someone on shoulder and say, "Dad, can I buy you a Coke?" That is code for, "You are making a scene and making it unpleasant for all the spectators." Taking Dad for a Coke may settle him down and give him a chance to understand the bigger picture. Parents will learn, if they are coached.

I will be
at your graduation
with great pride.

The Relationship Doesn't End

Graduation is a time that I love and hate. Selfishly I know I am not going to get to see some of these kids as much. I write the kids a message because I want them to have something in writing from Coach. I tell them they are being SENT now into the community to make a difference.* They have been prepared (to a degree) to go make a difference, and I expect them to do just that. With that said, we coaches still have more work to do. I let them know I expect an invitation to their college graduation, as well as their wedding. I have no clue if any other man in their life is planning on being at their graduation and wedding, but a Playmakers coach IS.

Some great conversations we coaches have had with our kids include what their kids are going to look like and be like. It is fun to have them think about those things. "Son, is *your* son going to be as big of a pain as you were?" Just getting our kids to talk is precious. At one breakfast, I was surprised when two of the three kids I was with told me they have been homeless before. Why did they share that with me? Because I told them it was their job to let me know who does not have a place to sleep or who is hungry. Now, how do you think I am going to coach or communicate with two kids who I know have been without a home?

Information like this is life changing. It can create a bond that will change us all. A kid is not going to tell you he has been homeless on a questionnaire. It comes on a Saturday morning, after a funeral, when you get into your pocket and buy breakfast and talk about making sure we are all in this together. I don't know what you did on that Saturday morning, but I had the privilege of being with my kids and mentoring Playmakers.

In the most real setting, we encourage our kids to set goals. They are setting life goals when we talk about things like graduation and what it will look like when they are Dads and Fathers.

Here is an interesting question, and a great conversation starter. Ask your player, "Son, what has one of our coaches taught you that you might want to teach *your* son?" Or, Coach, "What will *you* teach *your* freshmen next season?"

*This idea also came from Joe Ehrmann at that early morning breakfast back in 2005.

A band, a float, and homecoming: that's high school football.

Establish Traditions

One of the things that high school football can do is bring a community together. Grant High School is one of the state's ranked programs, yet it's in one of the most economically challenged areas in California. That community has such pride, and they love their Pacers. Coach Alberghini is a legend in that community. He has put his signature on that program. He has done more for kids of all colors than any politician in the city.

Too many kids are playing for the wrong reasons, and that can be fueled by the coach. I get excited when a recruiter comes from Cal or San Diego State (my alma mater), and the kids get all geeked up too. Truth is, for most of us coaches, a player who receives a scholarship does not come along very often.

I still love to hear a band and see the floats at the games. To me, that *is* high school football. I am an expert on homecoming and floats, because *everybody* wants to play us for their homecoming. (That will change soon.)

Our kids know that the band and cheerleaders work as hard as we do. We let them know regularly that we appreciate them. Some coaches believe that the school was built to support their football program, and some actually have been built for that reason. It is sad when those priorities get so far out of alignment.

A football program can change the culture of a campus, and we are actually doing that at Encina. Already, in my first year here, our kids are raising their grades across the board. We are cleaning the campus, serving in the community, and we have a relationship with Rotary. We were written about three times this season in the city's newspaper, because we are doing the right things. This is the same school that had its JV program cancelled after four games last year due to academic ineligibility. That's the difference the Playmakers program has made.

Coach, you can leave a fingerprint on the team and the school you coach by establishing traditions that stay long after you are gone. This year we took our team to Lake Tahoe for a weekend. For most of our kids, it was the first time they had seen snow or that huge lake. What a blast we had! We stayed in a lodge and talked all night. Another tradition at Tahoe is the Polar Bear Plunge. (Take a guess at who has to go first!) This experience was provided for us by a great bunch of men at our church who help support us. They're not trying to make a religious statement. They're just men who are willing to provide an experience of a lifetime for the kids. All of these activities have strengthened our relationships with organizations that now support Playmakers and Encina. It is just one of several traditions that we have begun.

Coach, start your traditions now.

There was no "quit"
in the firemen
on 9-11.

Get Inspired about Something

As you can tell, I love history, and 9-11 is burned into my memory banks. Like most of us, I remember exactly where I was when I heard about the first tower going down. I saw so many heroic acts. We can draw from those today. I cried watching people rally to help one another. I think that piece of history has so many uses on the football field.

I recall how those firemen worked to find *their* teammates. They would not quit, even after the game was declared over. Can you remember those guys working and digging and refusing to give up? Now, clearly understand that I do not want to try to compare the tragedy of 9-11 to a high school football game, but I have seen that same spirit in a young man named Pete Holman whose physical disabilities should have kept him from playing. Pete has the no-quit 9-11 spirit and heart that will not allow anything to keep him off the field. I love Pete Holman.

I remember very little about the Civil Rights Movement that shook our country in the 1960s, but I have played the game with men from the South.

I've seen firsthand the injustices that men and women have incurred. Our kids here have no reference point to life in the South, or why the Civil War was fought, and why that is such an important part of our American history.

At our team sleepovers, we try to broaden their understanding by watching movies that teach these important lessons. *Remember the Titans* is a great movie to show your kids! There are so many lessons in that movie, just as there are in *Rudy, We Are Marshall,* and *Friday Night Lights.*

Coach, the story of King Leonidas defending the path of Thermopylae in ancient Greece has tremendous lessons. The 300 Spartans who fought the Persians is an unbelievable story. So is the story of the explorer Cortez who, upon arriving on the shores of the enemy, ordered his Naval Commanders to burn their own ships. Then he turned to his men and said, "Men, we have no retreat. We win, or we die."

Some of us need to "burn our ships" and make a new commitment to these kids. We need to recruit committed men who will fight the cause alongside us. We need to be leaders who inspire others and make them want to be around us.

If your Mom calls me because she's having a problem with you, we're gonna go to the track and run.

An Unrewarded Hero

If Mom is having a problem with one of her kids, I get involved right away. Moms have my phone number, and I invite them to call me whenever they are feeling challenged. Kids rarely will try to play the same games with me that they play with Mom. If they tell Mom their homework is done, I will know if that is true on Monday morning. You see, Mom and I are a team. We are working together to get the job done.

Kids do not always give their single Moms the same courtesies as they give Auntie or Grammie. That is just the way it works. As a coach, I have the opportunity to help Mom and see to it that her son does not take advantage of her. Mom gets too little credit.

With our kids, sometimes Mom is not there at all, but if she is, she is going to be respected at all times. With all she is balancing, Mom deserves it. On more than one occasion, I have driven Mom to the food bank and stood in line with her so she can get groceries. I stand in line with Mom so her son knows they do not need to be embarrassed. It also keeps me humble and reminds me how blessed I am.

By God's grace, my family and I have always had enough to eat. I just go crazy thinking about how one of our kids has not eaten and may be hungry. The solution (be it only temporary) is a refrigerator in the weight room that always has peanut butter and jelly and bread in it.

If you are looking for a 100% approval rating, you are in the wrong business.

Who Do You Submit To?

Coach Tree is such a great sounding board for me. I will call him and tell him that I am having a problem with a parent who wants me fired for grade checking their son *too much*. This is true! Tree will remind me time and time again that he and I have trouble keeping our family of four happy some days. "What makes you think you can make fifty kids, and their families, and Administration all happy campers EVERY DAY?" We must pick our battles to die over, so die over integrity and character, not whether a dysfunctional couple likes you or not.

As a Head Coach, I have some wonderful assistant coaches who have permission to call me on integrity and character issues. *I submit to them.* Do you hear the word I am using here? *Submit* is a word we men do not like. When you are the Head Coach, you may begin to think you really are the boss. Do not fall into this trap. Keep men of character around you who will not let you get caught up in the moment.

We have a rule we call the "I have it, Coach" rule. It applies particularly to ME. As coaches, all of us have moments where we just have gone too far and are on a kid too hard. If it hasn't happened to you, it will. When one of my coaches observes this, he will step in and say, "I have it, Coach." This is the code that means I need to step away and cool down. I MUST submit to my assistant in this case. As a Head Coach, who do you submit to on the field? Who do you give permission to hold YOU accountable and keep your character in check? There are moments where your character is going to be challenged. Doing the right thing at the right moment is a must. As someone once said, "Iron sharpens iron."

When you are tough on a kid on the field, in our coaching vernacular that is sometimes called "blowing a kid up." If this happens, it is imperative that you not leave that kid thinking he is not good enough. A good coach will repair the "tear down" as soon as possible. (A great coach will not tear a kid down to begin with!) My assistants go to the kid quickly and coach that kid on the correction, whether it's football or a character breakdown. I am not talking about an X or O issue here, but the larger picture of strengthening the kid's character.

It might interest you to know we have freshmen entertainment night at Encina where the freshmen football players' job for the evening is to entertain the rest of the team. It is a fun, *no hazing* sleepover, and we have a blast. Usually the freshmen will do impersonations of the coaches. You can learn a lot about yourself, if you look closely. These kids, in a fun manner, will show you what you look like through their eyes. It can be quite an experience, if you allow them the opportunity to "critique" you in this non-threatening manner. A skit will tell you a lot more than the end-of-the-year evaluations you have them fill out!

Change your style if you need to.

Those Three Little Words

I don't ever remember a coach telling me that he loved me. I know that as a high school player, I was a coach's nightmare. I desperately wanted my varsity high school coach's approval. Today, when I see my old JV coach, Andy Braio, we hug. We tell each other how much we love each other, and when we see each other, we cry like two women watching *Steel Magnolias*.

I love my wife, Linda, with all my heart, but I find myself saying "I love you" more at practice than at home. I want my kids to hear a man say it. I want them to know it is okay for a man to say those words. I counsel with too many men today who did not hear those necessary words as a child. Today, a staggering number of the kids in our country live in a house without their biological father. (It's much higher in the inner city.) Who is telling those young men that they are loved? Who, that these kids believe in, is saying, "You are good enough, and I am proud of you"? It must be you, Coach! You may be all that they have!

You say that is not your style? You are just not a warm and fuzzy coach? Then let me ask you—what are you accomplishing by keeping these kids at a distance? A better winning percentage? Is this about you, or is it about that kid you are shaping? I love to watch Pete Carroll from USC on the sidelines. He is jumping up and down hugging any Trojan he can find. He is not afraid to show his affection for those kids.

You may have to change or alter your style. As coaches, we can do that if we need to. You are not too old; just get coached up on how to get it done.

I am fifty-two years old, and I do this exercise periodically. I challenge you to do the same. Hover over *your* funeral. Look down upon it, and just see the picture. Where is your win/loss record going to be displayed? Who is going to speak, and are they going to say, "Thank you, Coach, for keeping me at a distance, because that really molded me"? You have the opportunity to design that scene with one player after another lining up at the podium to talk about how you told them you loved them.

Show your kids what compassion means.

Help the Teachers Teach

There are numerous practical lessons that we teach on the field. Since we run a no-huddle offense, we hand signal in our plays like a lot of teams do. We incorporate "right brain creative memory" in our play calling, and that helps the kids in the classroom as well. It is so easy to teach creative memory that I am beginning to speak about it at different settings across the country. We draw comparisons between learning the plays and remembering history or algebra equations. As a person who has studied creative memory, I see the uses and applications in education, and we lay that same foundation using football as the classroom.

I like giving the kids terms they can use later. We ask the kids to be "vicarious learners," meaning they learn by watching others. The other day, a teacher stopped me and said one of my players told the class that they could do a better job by learning vicariously. We have told our defense that they are being "eviscerated" (many times). What we are telling them, of course, is that the offense is killing us.

I try to introduce a new word to the kids regularly. It has had quite an impact on the Administration. We're demonstrating our commitment to having our kids be student athletes. How much time does it take? Not much. It is just part of being a Playmakers coach. Give your kids words like *compassion, edify, relentless* (I like that one), *forgiveness, cognitive,* and many more. It will separate you, and it will solidify you with the teachers on campus.

I love the scene in *Remember the Titans* where a kid comes to his coach and hugs him and says, "I am going to college, Coach." Some kids in the inner city DO NOT believe that college is a possibility for them. That is just not acceptable. I have our Community College coaches come to our campus as often as I can get them there. Our kids don't need to worry about Pete Carroll from USC being on our campus. They need to know what a great logical step Community College is for most kids today. An AA (Associate Arts) degree is a great two-year first step, and I will celebrate our kids getting that one out of the way.

Coach, begin the process by teaching your kids what compassion means.

I can't be your Dad, but I'll sub for him if you need me to.

Begin Healing Wounds

I have a close friend whose daughter has not spoken to him in over five years, and he doesn't even know why. It is a painful story, and we are praying for their reunion. I hope someone in her life is championing her Dad and giving her a perspective that he cannot offer at this point in her life. I hope someone is telling her that her Dad loves her more than she can imagine.

That is what I try to do for kids who have broken relationships with their Dads. How can a hurting sixteen-year-old possibly process and unwind the scars of a broken home and a bad marriage? That child may or may not have any accurate reference point. As a coach, you can listen and be a voice for the future. Help your kids understand that how things appear today will *not* be forever.

I have a Playmaker who lost his Dad three years ago, and to this day, he cannot talk about it. All I can do is BE THERE when he is ready. This is a kid who graduated four years ago. He is in the Persian Gulf, and he still e-mails me when national security will allow him to. My job is not even close to being done with him.

Where are our kids learning forgiveness today? Most are coming from a broken home, and quite often, Mom has every right to be hurt. I am not too sure that a young man can process forgiveness when he has to figure it out all by himself. Be a legend, Coach! Step in and coach him through it! What kind of a man and Husband will that make him? Do you believe that forgiveness or unforgiveness factors into the 50% divorce rate today?

Coach, we are talking about subjects ranging from forgiveness, to divorce rates, to broken homes, to single Moms. You may or may not have signed up for all that, but if not you, *who* is going to get it done? I have attended two funerals in the last three months. At both of these funerals, the person who presided over one and spoke at the second was a high school football coach.

*Let's begin
a legacy together.*

What Will You Leave Behind?

There are words that I just love, and *legacy* is one of them. One of the definitions of a legacy is, "Something handed down from an ancestor, or a predecessor, or from the past." I tell our kids that someday they will be a coach, and then we laugh about that. Some actually have come back to assist, and I find it funny when they say, "Coach, were we that hard to coach?"

We need some crazy men with their hair on fire, as well as quiet steady men, to create legacies and finish this job. This character mission of helping young men enter manhood with a good Game Plan will take rebels who are not afraid to howl at the moon. What is it going to look like when we have men out there who are not watered down, milk toast, safe guys coaching our young men? Playmakers coaches will create a legacy, because we are men of influence with kids who will listen and execute the play we have created.

Bill McCartney was the coach of the University of Colorado Buffaloes when he left a nationally prestigious job to create the legacy of Promise Keepers. He has stadiums filled with men who aspire to be better men using

Christian principles. What a risk he took in resigning his football career to chase his calling of a much larger story! I admire what Coach Mac has done in creating a legacy of men who keep one another accountable as Husbands and Fathers.

Look into the crystal ball and see these men who you have influenced over the years. Coaches, we are going to do something about the fatherless rate. We can take this winless team of a divorce rate and turn it around. Tell me where else it is going to get done. I am not too sure MTV is concerned about it. Let's give that legacy to these young men who need us now more than ever. Have your kids do some research on who Coach Mac is at the library, and let's create a legacy together.

In Conclusion

Coach, there is a challenge that I would like to put in front of you. Very few of us will win a state title, and your youth football record is not going to be mentioned at your funeral. As I've already said, what will they say about you when you are gone? What legacy will you leave? My good friend, Tree, will have kids who will speak about him picking them up at 6 a.m. for early tutoring, and how he cared for them with tough love. These are the things they will talk about, and not his record.

I invite you to get with a coach, or a man whom you trust, and have a deep conversation about WHY you coach, and do your values and actions match up to why you do it? Have a friend who will bring you hard truth about how you interact with kids. Do you have a relationship with someone who will speak to you that way? The question is, are you coachable and capable of transformation? Of course you are. You just have to assess if it is worth the effort. I promise you that it is. The possibilities are endless. You may find that this moves you into a new direction, possibly even a new vocation, and wakes you up to finish life well.

We are a strong body of coaches and kids. We are difference makers who will coach kids to become great Husbands and Fathers and leaders of character. We can teach them to finish the game, and I mean the game of life.

By coaching in this manner, you may find healing in scars you have carried and don't even realize that you have them. Tell me what platform is dealing with the skyrocketing divorce rate, or that kids are living without the male influence they are starving for? Who is going to get it done, the youth group at church? Or MTV? Is it in the next version of video games like Madden? No, it is on our shoulders. Our platform is the football field. We have leverage with these kids because they want to play the best game in the world. Playmakers offers coaches' clinics, football camps, blogs, and corporate resources. Now we need you to step up and coach these kids with life skills.

Are you in the drill?

Greg "Coach Roz" Roeszler

Partnering with Playmakers

Playmakers is an organization of coaches, teachers, mentors, and everyday people who genuinely care about the welfare of today's young people. We work together, each in our own way, to help children become responsible citizens of tomorrow. While our outreach embraces all children, our focus is especially on disadvantaged at-risk children, kids who have had a tough beginning in life and who are in need of guidance, support, and encouragement. As Playmakers, we strive to give these kids a Game Plan to follow so they can reach beyond their present circumstances and realize their dreams.

Playmakers is run entirely through the donations of its supporters. Because of the generosity of people who care, we are able to offer our Coaching Clinics and our Summer Football Camps without charge to the participants. Donations are always gratefully accepted.

The Playmakers program began in the Sacramento area. From there it spread throughout California and is now reaching not only a national but also an international audience. There are many ways to be part of this rapidly growing program.

If you'd like to volunteer in some capacity, or contribute whatever special talent you have in your own unique way, please know we would welcome it. Just let us know what you have in mind, and we'll find a way to plug you in.

As Playmakers, we mentor high-risk youth, using coaching and sports as a vehicle. This philosophy can be applied in a variety of settings, including music and the arts. If that is your forte, let us know. We'd be happy to help you get the Playmakers program up and running.

Playmakers is made up of many hands, many hearts, and many willing feet. We invite you to be among us.

Coach Roz Roeszler, (916) 220-1284
E-mail: CoachRoz@ThePlaymakers.org
Web site: *www.ThePlaymakers.org*
Blog: *www.ThePlaymakers.org/blog*

Invite Coach Roz to Speak to Your Group

Coach Roz welcomes the opportunity to speak to groups anywhere, any time. His dynamic, heartfelt presentations have a way of enabling his listeners to see possibilities they have not previously considered, and helps them find the means within themselves to reach a little higher, be a little stronger.

Coach Roz frequently speaks on a variety of subjects at corporate functions, before both civic and faith-based groups, as well as youth leadership seminars and churches. His talks to sales and business management teams open new horizons for his listeners, making it easier for them to "think outside the box."

Coach Roz has also had great success speaking at group homes. His presentations are laced with humor and underscored with compassion and sensitivity to the needs of his listeners, whether they are staff or residents.

Roz has a special gift of being able to reach the hearts of even the most troubled children, leaving them with a feeling of validation and worth they may not have felt before. His ability to communicate with even the most withdrawn of children is remarkable, just as is his ability to bring hope and possibility to adults in group homes and rehabilitation centers. In addition, Roz is able to give the staff at these centers a fresh perspective both on their work and their life.

When you invite Coach Roz to speak to your group, he becomes part of your team, and you of his. To bring Coach Roz to your group, or your area, he can be reached through any of these links:

Coach Roz Roeszler, (916) 220-1284
E-mail: CoachRoz@ThePlaymakers.org
Web site: *www.ThePlaymakers.org*
Blog: *www.ThePlaymakers.org/blog*

Attend a
Coaching for Character Clinic

All across the country, our cities are filled with fatherless children. The residual effects of this fatherless society are beyond our comprehension, yet there is hope. Coach Roz is calling on our coaches to stand up and teach our children to be real heroes by becoming people who can be counted on. Roz's clinics give coaches a roadmap for building character that they can use with the kids back home. Roz shows them how to make life safer for these children. He teaches coaches how to be there for the long haul, so they can set an example the kids will not forget.

In addition to coaching techniques, these one-day clinics show coaches how to communicate with both kids and coaches in an effective and positive manner. The purpose of these clinics is to show people how to coach for the larger purpose of building a life, and not "just" to have a winning team. Character-based leadership, responsible citizenship, and team building are just a few of the topics that are covered. These clinics bring coaches, team captains, and team leaders together where they can share their concerns, ask their questions, and then work together toward their common goal.

Through these clinics, Coach Roz and his staff are developing an ever-broadening network of support both for coaches and for the underprivileged kids they work with. Volunteer coaches from both high school and college levels assist in running the clinics and camps.

Each summer, Roz's Clinic for Parents offers specific tools that help them help their children through the difficult growing years.

Playmakers also serves as a Coach's Certification Center, providing the hours needed for Youth Coaching Certification.

All of our clinics are funded by private donations and corporate sponsorships. If you would like to bring a Coaching Clinic to your area, or if you would like to learn more about this unique way of coaching, contact Coach Roz.

Coach Roz Roeszler, (916) 220-1284
E-mail: CoachRoz@ThePlaymakers.org
Web site: *www.ThePlaymakers.org*
Blog: *www.ThePlaymakers.org/blog*

Free Playmakers Summer Camps

Coach Roz and his dedicated team of assistants hold free summer camps for football and other sports all over the State of California for children from ages seven through high school. With enough advance notice, he will run camps anywhere else in the country. The camps are coordinated with local coaches, as well as with coaches who travel from other states to help with this outreach. At these camps, children not only have a chance to learn important skills in their sport, they are also coached on what "real" character is, and what it means to be a responsible member of your family and your community. In other words, Playmakers is training the next generation of leaders by teaching young student athletes about themselves, their potential, and how to serve others.

In exchange, the children are expected to maintain good grades in school. They are also required to perform community service as a group, under the guidance of the coaches. The results have been startling. Kids who before were fighting, simply because they were born on different streets, have learned that they all have the same hopes and dreams, and even more, that they can become friends.

Coach Roz also holds Youth Quarterback Camps where young quarterbacks can learn specialized skills and receive leadership training.

If you'd like to have a Playmakers camp in your area, we would need a "core" person to organize pre-camp activities, find volunteers, and connect Coach Roz with leaders in your community. Having a "core" person is key to our being able to come to a new area.

Volunteers are a necessary component at our camps. We need people to help with registration and check in. We need people to set up the field and man the water station. We always need a First Aid person and a trainer. We need a liaison who can link our efforts with the local law enforcement and the Fire Department. People can also contribute by donating food and other supplies, and making donations to help with the ongoing cost of these camps. All of our camps are funded by private donations and corporate sponsorships.

Together, we are making a difference. The world of tomorrow is in our children's hands. What better way to assure them a promising future than to teach them skills that will empower them for a lifetime!

Inquire about bringing a Playmakers Summer Football or other Sports Camp to your area by contacting Coach Roz. He would welcome your call.

Coach Roz Roeszler, (916) 220-1284
E-mail: CoachRoz@ThePlaymakers.org
Web site: *www.ThePlaymakers.org*
Blog: *www.ThePlaymakers.org/blog*

About Playmakers' Books

Greg "Coach Roz" Roeszler has dedicated his life to helping under-privileged, at-risk children, wherever they are. These books were born out of that passion. Written with wisdom, humor, and deep compassion, each book is certain to touch the heart of its readers. The insights contained within these books apply to every aspect of life, not just the game of football. The books not only speak directly to their targeted audience, they offer deep insight to a general audience as well.

Coach Roz works closely with the Mothers of his students, many of whom are single parents in need of guidance and encouragement. Roz makes a point of forming a team with these Moms not only to help them, but ultimately to help their child as well. Over time, Roz developed a repertoire of sayings that he used with his Moms. It was a natural extension for him to collect those sayings and put them in a book so they could be used as a reference. Thus, *Raising Your Teenage Athlete, A Playbook for Moms,* was born.

Many of the children Roz works with come from extremely difficult circumstances. Some are homeless, or parent-less, or father-less. Their story needs to be told, and solutions must be provided. Roz believes that at least some of the answers can be found within the kids themselves. Through the game of football, Roz teaches the kids to be accountable to each other and to care about each other by being part of the football family. Slowly the kids have learned what it means to be a responsible citizen of their community, to help and serve others, and to reach beyond themselves simply because it is the right thing to do.

After seeing the difference this approach made with his own students, Coach Roz began working with coaches all over the State of California, teaching them how to coach character while coaching football. As his clinics increased in number, so did the need for a Coaching for Character manual. In his own unique way, Coach Roz shows his readers how to focus on the deeper values that lie hidden within the game. It is Roz's premise that, when taught correctly, the game of football can be a blueprint for life. *Coaching for a Bigger Win, A Playbook for Coaches,* contains that blueprint, at least in part.

These books, written out of the abundance of Roz's heart, come from a man who has been able to connect with a larger vision for his life. It is his hope, and his prayer, that those who read these books will be guided to find a larger vision for their own life as well.

Order Form

Coaching for a Bigger Win, A Playbook for Coaches

Price: $12.95 x _____ (number of copies) $ _____

Case: $300 x _____ (number of cases) 24 books per case $ _____

Sales Tax (7% when shipped to Nebraska addresses only) $ _____

Shipping & Handling: $5.00 per book, $25 per case

Raising Your Teenage Athlete, A Playbook for Moms

Price: $12.95 x _____ (number of copies) $ _____

Case: $300 x _____ (number of cases) 24 books per case $ _____

Sales Tax (7% when shipped to Nebraska addresses only) $ _____

Shipping & Handling: $5.00 per book, $25 per case

Customer Name: _____

Shipping Address:_____

City:_____ State: _____ Zip:_____

Telephone: (_____) _____

Email: _____

Payment Method:

□ Visa   □ Master Card   □ American Express   □ Discover

Name on Card _____

Billing Address (if different from above) _____

City:_____ State: _____ Zip:_____

Card Number_____ CVV_____

Signature _____Exp. Date_____

Mail This Form To:

Playmakers Press

c/o CMI Fulfillment

13518 L St., Omaha, NE 68137

E-mail: playmakers@conciergemarketing.com

Or order online at: *www.ThePlaymakers.org*

Authors (Left to Right): Donna Miesbach, David Humm and Greg Roeszler

About the Authors

Greg Roeszler's athletic career includes being a quarterback/punter at the University of Minnesota and San Diego State, as well as a camp quarterback with the Oakland Raiders in 1980. His passion for lost and forgotten kids led him to leave a successful career as a sales and management trainer so he could devote his life to working with at-risk kids. As Greg puts it, "I am a High School Football Coach, a Husband and Dad struggling to be the man I have been called to be." Out of that calling, Playmakers Mentoring Foundation was born. Supported early on by a network of coaches and friends who shared his vision, Playmakers now reaches throughout the State of California, and is beginning to emerge on the national and international scene as well.

You can learn more about this amazing outreach on their web site, *www.ThePlaymakers.org.*

Greg, his wife, Linda, and their two daughters live in Sacramento, California.

For almost thirty years, **Donna Miesbach's** inspirational poems and articles have reached around the globe through such venues as *Unity Magazine, Daily Word, Chicken Soup for the Teenage Soul II, Ideals,* and the *Cup of Comfort* book series. She was also a featured author in *Wise Women Speak, 20 Ways to Turn Stumbling Blocks into Stepping Stones.*

In 1985, Donna was named Inspirational Poet of the Year by *The Poet Magazine.* Her collection of poems, *Trails of Stardust, Poems of Inspiration and Insight,* was published in 2002. Some of her poems have also been published as choral anthems.

In addition to her work as an author, Donna was certified as a meditation and yoga instructor by Dr. Deepak Chopra. She has an active teaching practice, which reaches into several Midwestern States. You can learn more about Donna on her web site, *www.DonnaMiesbach.com.*

Donna is a retired organist and resides in Omaha, Nebraska.

David Humm knows football like the back of his hand. More than that, he knows what it takes to be a quality player both on and off the field. David was one of the University of Nebraska's most outstanding quarterbacks, setting records from 1972–74 that still have not been broken.

After receiving numerous prestigious awards, he spent the next ten years in the NFL where he played for the Oakland/L.A. Raiders, the Buffalo Bills, and the Baltimore Colts. It was as a Raider that David and his team won the Super Bowl XVIII and Super Bowl XXI Championships.

For the last fourteen seasons, David has been the co-host of the Oakland Raiders pre- and post-game shows for the Oakland Raiders Radio Network and is affectionately known by millions as one of the Voices of the Raiders Radio Broadcasts.

David lives and works in Las Vegas, Nevada.